Edward Duffield Neill

**Notes on the Virginia Colonial Clergy**

Edward Duffield Neill

**Notes on the Virginia Colonial Clergy**

ISBN/EAN: 9783337155209

Printed in Europe, USA, Canada, Australia, Japan

Cover: Foto ©ninafisch / pixelio.de

More available books at **www.hansebooks.com**

ON THE

# VIRGINIA COLONIAL CLERGY.

BY

## EDWARD D. NEILL,

PRESBYTER OF REFORMED EPISCOPAL CHURCH.

REPRINTED FROM EPISCOPAL RECORDER.

PHILADELPHIA:
1220 SANSOM STREET.
1877.

*Extract from Sermon of Patrick Copland, before the Virginia Company, preached at Bow Church, London, Thursday, April* 18. 1622.

" And, that I may bend my speech unto all, seeing so many of the Lord's worthies have done worthily in this noble action ; yea, and seeing that some of them greatly rejoice in this, that God hath enabled them to help forward this glorious work, both with their prayers and with their purses, let it be your grief and sorrow to be exempted from the company of so many honorable-minded men, and from this noble plantation, tending so highly to the advancement of the Gospel, and to the honoring of our dread Sovereign, by enlarging of his kingdoms, and adding a fifth crown unto his other four : for ' *En dat Virginia quintam* ' is the motto of the legal seal of Virginia."

# VIRGINIA COLONIAL CLERGY.

## CHAPTER I.

### CHAPLAINS OF EARLY EXPEDITIONS.

Edward Maria Wingfield, the President of the First Council of Virginia, makes the following statement, relative to the first clergyman who arrived, in 1607, with the founders of Jamestown:—

### REV. ROBERT HUNT.

"For my first worke, which was to make right choice of a spiritual pastor, I appealed to the remembrance of my Lo. of Caunt., his Grace, who gave me very gracious audience in my request. And the world knoweth when I took with me truly a man, in my opinion, not any waie to be touched with the rebellious humor of a papist spirit, nor blemished with the least suspicion of a factious schismatic."

The appointment of Robert Hunt as chaplain of Newport's expedition to Virginia came through the direct agency of Richard Hakluyt, Prebend of Westminster, who was an earnest advocate for the planting of an English colony in America.

Anderson supposes that he had been a rector in Kent, before he received the position of chaplain. Amid all the dissensions of the first colonists, he proved himself a gentle shepherd, and won the respect of all classes. President Wingfield speaks of him as follows: "Two or three Sunday mornings the Indians gave us alarms; by that times they were answered, the place about us well discovered, and our divine service ended, the day was far spent. The preacher did ask me if it were my pleasure to have a sermon; he said he was prepared for it. I made answer, that our men were weary and hungry, and that he did see the time of the day far spent (for at other times he never made such question, but the service finished, he began his sermon), and that if it pleased him, we would spare him till some other time. I never failed to take such notes, by writing, out of his doctrine as my capacity would comprehend, unless some rainy day hindered my endeavors."

On rainy days the place of worship was not very comfortable. The congregation assembled in fair weather under an old sail, suspended from trees, but when it rained service was held in a rotten tent. In time the colonists constructed a barn-like edifice, with a roof of turf and earth resting upon rafters, and in this place, as humble as the manger of Bethlehem, Hunt officiated as long as he lived.

In the winter of 1609 a fire broke out, which destroyed Hunt's library, and before the summer of 1609 he had died, but the precise time has not been ascertained.

### REV. MR. GLOVER.

In June, A. D. 1611, Sir Thomas Gates left England on a second voyage to Virginia. William Crashaw, the celebrated divine, father of the poet, says that the Rev. Mr. Glover accompanied him, who had been "an approved preacher in Bedford and Huntingdonshire, a graduate of Cambridge, reverenced and respected," but he soon died.

Crashaw writes, "He endured not the sea-sickness of the countrey so well as younger and stronger bodies; and so, after zealous and faithful performance of his ministeriall dutie, whilest he was able, he gave his soule to Christ Jesus (under whose banner he went to fight, and for whose glorious name's sake, he undertook the danger) more worthy to be accounted a true confessor of Christ than hundreds that are canonized in the Pope's Marytyrologie."

ALEXANDER WHITAKER, MINISTER AT HENRICO, VIRGINIA, A. D. 1611-1617.

Crashaw, the father of the poet, and a distinguished divine, in the year 1613, alludes to the ministers who had gone to America as able and fit men, "all of them graduates, allowed preachers, single men, having no pastoral cares, nor charge of children," and exhorts them in these words: "Though Satan visibly and palpably reigns there, more than in any other known place in the world, yet be of courage, blessed brethren; God will tread Satan under your feet shortly, and the ages to come will eternize your names, as the apostles of Virginia." Among these so-called apostles, one who came with Sir Thomas Dale, in 1611, was Alexander Whitaker. He had been comfortably settled in the north of England for five or six years, after graduating at Cambridge, when he tore himself away from comforts and friends, and "his warm nest," constrained by the love of Christ to become a missionary. He was the son of the great scholar, William Whitaker, for many years Professor of Divinity, and Master of St. John's College, Cambridge, of whom a poet said: "He was the shield of truth, the scourge of error." With his father he held the then prevailing opinions of the Church of England. He taught that a bishop and presbyter in the New Testament were of the same order, and that the only Apostolical Succession was based upon the presentation of Scriptural truths. "If," said the elder Whitaker, "he is a perfect minister who has learned the scriptural doctrine, and explained it to the people, then that is a true and perfect Church which receives and cherishes such doctrine."

The son had been taught, also, that baptism purifies none, except those who receive the promise of gratuitous justification in Christ, and that there was nothing like a real, express presence in the elements upon the Lord's Table.

But one of Alexander Whitaker's sermons was published. In 1613 it was printed in London, and contains the following sentence:—

"Let not the servants of superstition, that think to merit by their good works, go beyond us in well-doing, neither let them be able to open their mouths against us, and to condemn the religion of our Protestation, for want of charitable deeds."

Sir Thomas Dale had passed many years among the Presbyterians of Holland, before coming to Virginia. His first wife was a relative, and his second wife a sister of Sir W. Throckmorton, a man of Puritan affinities. Many of the settlers at Henrico were Dutchmen, and it was to be expected that Whitaker's views would be in sympathy with Low-Churchmen, the prevailing party among the people of England.

Hamor, the secretary of the Colony, in a narrative published in London, in 1615, prints a letter of Whitaker's, written in June, 1614, which contains the earliest account of a church organization among the English of North America. He writes: "Every Sabbath day we preach in the forenoon, and catechize in the afternoon. Every Saturday, at night, I exercise in Sir Thomas Dale's house. Our Church affairs be consulted on by the Minister and four of the most religious men. Once every month we have a communion, and once a year a solemn fast."

The weekly religious service, or exercise, on Saturday night, was a characteristic of the Puritans within the Church of England. Purchas states that the surplice was not even spoken of in Whitaker's parish. The consultation with four of the most religious men resembled a Dutch consistory.

Before June, 1617, Whitaker was drowned, and William Wickham, a pious man, without Episcopal ordination, conducted the services at Henrico. In 1621 Rev. Jonas Stockton took charge of the parish.

The unreliable John Smith published a letter, purporting to have been written by the Rev. Jonas Stockham, on May 20th, 1621, which Purchas states was addressed to Alexander Whitaker. Alluding to the Indians, he remarks: "We have sent boys among them to learn their language, but they return worse than they went: but I am no statesman, nor love I to meddle with anything but my books, but I can find no probability by this course to draw them to goodness; and I am persuaded if Mars and Minerva go hand-in-hand, they will effect more good in one hour, than these verbal Mercurians in their lives. And till their Priests and Ancients have their throats cut, there is no hope to bring them to conversion."

This sentiment, attributed to Stockham, we find in almost similar language in a letter written on April 15th, 1609, by the historiographer, Richard Hakluyt, to the Virginia Company. His words relative to the Indians are, "They be also as unconstant as the weathercock, and most ready to take all occasions to do mischief. They are great liars and dissemblers, for which faults oftentimes they had their deserved payments. And many times they gave good testimonies of their great valor and resolution. To handle them gently, while gentle courses may be found to serve, it will be without comparison the best; but if gentle polishing will not serve, the one shall not want hammerers and rough masons enow—I mean our old soldiers trained up in the Netherlands—to square and prepare them to our preachers' hands."

No such letter could have been written to Whitaker, as alleged, in 1621, for in 1617 he was drowned. There was no Rev. Jonas Stockham in Virginia, but in 1620 there arrived, in the "Bona Nova," the Rev. Jonas Stockton, about thirty-six years of age, with a son Timothy, ten years old, and for a time he was minister at Henrico and New Bermudas.

At the instance of Sir William Throckmorton, in 1620, one of the Indian girls brought to London by Sir Thomas Dale in 1616, being weak with consumption, was sent to the house of a cousin of Whitaker, the Rev. William Gouge, who "took great pains to comfort her, both in soul and body." Gouge was a Cambridge graduate, noted for scholarship, oratory, piety and philanthropy. He was a member of the Westminster Assembly of Divines, and died in December, 1653, after a pastorate of forty-five years at Black Friars, London.

---

# CHAPTER II.

## CLERGY FROM A.D. 1619 TO A.D. 1630.

Hunt, Glover, and Whitaker had all been summoned to the "better land" before the assembling at Jamestown, on July 30th, 1619, of the first American legislature.

### RICHARD BUCK, CHAPLAIN OF THE "SEA VENTURE."

Richard Buck, who had been an Oxford student, was "an able and painful preacher," commended to honest Sir Thomas Gates by Bishop Ravis, of London, one of the translators of the King James' version of the Bible, a prelate of mildness and liberality.

He embarked in 1609, in the "Sea Venture," with Gates, Somers, and Captain Newport, and during a violent storm in the last days of July, the ship was wrecked at Bermudas. Here the passengers and sailors remained several months, and Buck was faithful in the discharge of his duties.

Strachey, Secretary of Virginia, says :— During our time of abode upon these islands, we had every Sunday two sermons preached by our minister, besides every morning and evening, at the ringing of a bell, we repaired all to public prayer, at what time the names of our whole company were called, and such as were wanting were duly punished." He was occupied while there in baptizing, burying, and marrying.

John Rolfe, whose name has become distinguished as the first man who established a tobacco plantation in Virginia, and linked with the romance about Pocahontas, was, with his white wife, passenger on the "Sea Venture." Mrs. Rolfe gave birth to a daughter, and on the 4th of February, 1609-10, she was christened Bermuda ; Strachey and Captain Newport standing as "witnesses." After a brief existence the child was buried on the Island.

A ship of seventy tons, named the "Deliverance," having been built, in it, and a small pinnace, called the "Patience," the party left, and in the latter part of May, 1610, arrived at Jamestown. Sir Thomas Gates, before he unrolled his commission and commenced his duties as Governor, caused the bell to be rung, and then the emaciated and desponding colonists listened to the "zealous and sorrowful prayer of Mr. Buck." On Sunday, the 10th of June, Lord Delaware arrived as Governor General, and immediately went ashore and heard "a sermon made by Mr. Buck." The church in which this sermon was preached a chronicle of that day described as "a homely thing, like a barn set upon crutchets, covered with rafts, sedge and earth ; so was also the walls."

Lord Delaware ordered the church to be repaired, and when completed it was twenty-four by sixty feet in dimensions, the pews made of cedar, the communion table of black walnut, a baptismal font hollowed out of a log like a canoe, and two bells on the west gable.

Every Sunday two sermons were delivered by Buck, or Glover, or Whitaker ; and the Puritan custom of a sermon or lecture ou Thursday was also observed. During the services, if present, Lord Delaware sat in the chancel, in a green velvet chair. Ill health soon compelled Delaware to go back to England, and then the rude church again began to decay.

Crashaw speaks of all the clergymen who left England, as being "single men." If this statement is correct, Buck must have married some of the female passengers wrecked at Bermudas, or some one in Virginia, soon after, for in 1611 there is evidence that he was a husband. Toward the latter part of that year, in the midst of great destitution, his wife bore a daughter, which was appropriately named Mara. The mother, in her desolation, thought, no doubt, of the green hedges and good cheer of dear old England, and appreciated the language of Naomi, in the Book of Ruth—"Call me not Naomi, call me Mara, for the Almighty hath dealt very bitterly with me. I went out full, and the Lord hath brought me home again, empty."

Three years after Mara's birth the Lord gave the wife of Buck a son, which was named Gershom. The good man thought of Moses, no doubt, who, when his wife, Zipporah, bare him a son, "he called his name Gershom, for, he said, I have been a stranger in a strange land."

In the year 1616, the minister's wife became the mother of a son, which proved a child of sorrow, and was well called Benoni. He did not chuckle and laugh in childish glee, he had a vacant stare, and it was soon evident that he would not be able to measure a yard of cloth, number twenty, or rightly name the days of the week, and that he, under the English Statute, would be called "a natural fool."

The fourth child was born about the time that the first legislature met, and the colony was "pelegged," or divided into many election precincts, and the boy was named Peleg.

Mr. Buck died before the year 1624, but the precise time has not been ascertained. Ambrose Harmar, who in 1645 was a member of the legislature from Jamestown, in a petition presented in 1637, states that he had for thirteen years had the care of the idiot Benoni Buck, the first in the colony, and appears to have been the guardian of the other children.

By Buck's will, his wife had a life interest in his lands, and after her death they were to belong to the children. Hening's Statutes state that the attention of the legislature of March 1654-5 was called to the will of Richard Buck, and it was decided that his lands descended to his children, and not to Bridget Bromfield, late wife of John Burrowes, and that Elizabeth Crompe was to remain in possession.

Thomas Crompe came to Virginia as early as A.D. 1624, and was a delegate to the legislature that met in February, 1631-32, from James City. Elizabeth Crompe may have been the daughter of Thomas Crompe and Mara Buck, and the grandchild of Rev. Richard Buck.

In 1624 Mara Buck, then unmarried, was living with John and Bridget Burrowes, at James City. Could Bridget Burrowes have been the widow of Buck, and, after the death of Burrowes, could Mr. Bromfield have become a third husband?

### GEORGE KEITH.

A minister named George Keith, thirty-three years of age, with a wife, and son John, aged six years, in 1617 arrived in the ship "George," and settled at Elizabeth City. He may have been the same person who was the first minister at the Bermudas, whose governor at this time was Daniel Tucker, who had been a councillor and prominent citizen of Virginia.

He entered one hundred acres, by patent, and for some time a creek in the neighborhood of Elizabeth City, now Hampton, was called Keith's.

His wife appears to have died, 1621. It

he was the first minister of Bermudas, he was a nonconformist.

### WILLIAM MEASE.

William Mease came about the time of Glover and Buck, remained ten years in Virginia, and in 1623 was living in England.

### THOMAS BARGRAVE.

Thomas Bargrave, who came in 1618, was the nephew of Dr. Bargrave, the Dean of Canterbury, and came out with his uncle, Captain John Bargrave, who spent several thousand pounds, with a Mr. Ward, in establishing a plantation on the south side of the James, above Martin Brandon, in the district through which runs a creek, to this day called Ward's. He probably succeeded Wickham at Henrico, and Whitaker at Bermuda Hundred. He died in 1621, and left his library, valued at one hundred marks, or seventy pounds, to the projected college at Henrico.

### DAVID SANDS, OR SANDYS.

David Sands, or Sandys, came in the "Bona Ventura," in 1620, and first dwelt at John Utie's plantation in Hog Island, but early in 1625 he was at the plantation of Captain Samuel Matthews, within the precincts of James City. In July, 1624, he petitioned for relief from calumny derogatory to his profession.

### JONAS STOCKTON

Arrived in January, 1621, in the ship "Bona Nova," and was about thirty-six years of age. His residence was at Elizabeth City, but for a time he preached at Henrico. In January, 1625, he was alive, but after this he is not mentioned in any of the records we have examined.

Governor Yeardley, in the spring of 1619, found a "poor ruinated church" at Henrico, and at Jamestown "a church built wholly at the charge of the inhabitants of that city, of timber, being fifty foot in length and twenty foot in breadth."

In 1621 Sir Francis Wyatt became Governor, and a number of clergymen came to Virginia, but the General Assembly of 1623 stated that "divers had no orders."

### ROBERT PAULET.

Robert Paulet, in July, 1621, was announced as one of the Governor's Council, and was at that time residing at Martin's Hundred. He had been engaged in 1619 to go to Southampton Hundred, founded by Tracy, Throckmorton, Thorp and others, in the triple capacity of "preacher, physician, and surgeon," and arrived in the month of December. He never took the oath of Councillor. The Virginia Company of London, in a letter dated July 22d, 1622, to Governor Wyatt writes, "Mr. Robert Paulet, the minister, was he whom the court chose to be of the Council; the adventurers of Martin's Hundred desire that he might be spared for that office, their business requiring his presence continually." *

### ROBERT BOLTON.

In the records of the London Company is found the following minute :—" Upon the Right Honorable the Earl of Southampton's recommendations of Mr. Bolton, minister, for his honesty and sufficiency in learning, and to undertake the care and charge of the ministry, the Company have been pleased to entertain him for their minister in some vacant place in Virginia."

Mr. Bolton came with Governor Wyatt, in October, 1621, and was sent to Elizabeth City. He was engaged by the planters of the eastern shore of the Chesapeake Bay, as their first minister, and preached for two years there, and perhaps a longer period. He may have been the Robert Bolton who, in 1609, took the degree of A. B. at Oxford.

On November 21st, 1623, Governor Wyatt issued the following :—

" WHEREAS, it is ordered that Mr. Bolton, minister, shall receive for his salary,

this year, throughout all the plantations at the Eastern Shore, ten pounds of tobacco and one bushel of corn for every planter and tradesman, above the age of sixteen years, alive at the crop: these are to require Captain William Epps, commander of the said plantation, to raise the said ten pounds of tobacco and one bushel of corn," etc.

### HAWTE WYATT.

Hawte Wyatt, named after his maternal grandfather, Sir W. Hawte, also came in October, 1621, in the same vessel with his brother, Gov. Wyatt. On the 16th of July, a few days after Bolton's appointment, it was signified to the London Company that Sir Francis Wyatt's brother, "being a Master of Arts, and a good divine, and very willing to go with him this present voyage, might be entertained and placed as Minister over his people, and have the same allowance towards the furnishing of himself with necessaries, as others have had; and that his wife might have her transport free, which motive was thought very reasonable," and it was ordered that he should have the same allowance as that which had been granted to Mr. Bolton.

It is probable that the minister's wife went back in the summer of 1623, as a companion of the Governor's wife, and in 1626 he came to England, his father having died. Upon his return to England he found a great deal of ecclesiastical controversy, and his sympathies were with the Puritans. Opposed to the retrogressions of Archbishop Laud, he was arraigned before the High Commission. On the 3d of October he became Vicar of Bexley, Kent, the seat of his ancestors. He was twice married, and on the 31st of July, 1638, died. Some of his descendants came back to Virginia. Anthony Wyatt, one of Governor Berkeley's councillors in 1642, may have been his son, and perhaps Ralph Wyatt, who married the widow of Captain William Button, a gentleman who had received from the Privy Council of England a grant of 7000 acres on both sides of the river Appomattox.

### WILLIAM BENNETT.

About the same time, in 1621, that Hawte Wyatt came, arrived William Bennett, in the ship "Sea Flower." He preached at the plantation settled under the auspices of Edward Bennett, a prominent London merchant, in the Warosquoyak district, which extended on the south side of James river. There is a warrant dated November 20th, 1623, for collecting of the estate of Robert Bennett the salary of William Bennett for two years.

His wife came in the "Abigail," in July, 1622, and shortly after his marriage, toward the close of the year 1624, he died.

On the 22d of January, 1624-5, Catharine, the widow of the minister, aged twenty-four, was residing at Shirley, with William, her infant, three weeks old.

### THOMAS WHITE.

In December, 1621, Thomas White arrived in the ship Warwick. Governor Wyatt and Council, in a letter to the London Company, written the next month, uses these words:—"The information given you of the want of worthy ministers here is very true, and therefore we must give you great thanks for sending out Mr. Thomas White. It is our earnest request that you would be pleased to send us out many more learned and sincere ministers, of which there is so great want in so many parts of the country."

White appears to have died before 1624, and his place of residence in the colony has not been ascertained.

### WILLIAM LEATE OR LEAKE.

Humphry Slany, one of the prominent merchants of London, at one of the meetings of the London Company in 1622, informed them that Mr. Leate, a man of "civil and good carriage," formerly a preacher in New Foundland, was desirous to go to Virginia, and would put the Company to no charge, except for necessaries and such books as should be useful to him. A committee conferred with him, and asked him to preach

on a certain Sunday, in the afternoon, on the second verse of the 9th chapter of Isaiah, at Saint Scythe's Church, which was surrounded by handsome mansions in Saint Swithen's lane, near London Stone.

He appears to have made a favorable impression. In a letter to the colonial authorities, the Company write, on 10th of July, 1622, O. S.:—"We send over Mr. William Leate, a minister recommended unto us for sufficiency of learning and integrity of life." In less than six months he died. Governor Wyatt, the next January, wrote: "The little experience we have of Mr. Leate made good your commendations of him, and his death to us very grievous."

### GREVILLE POOLEY.

Greville Pooley arrived in the ship "James," in 1622, and resided on the south side of James river, at Fleur-dieu Hundred, one of Governor Yeardley's plantations, adjoining Jordan's plantation.

Samuel Jordan, a few months after Pooley's arrival, died, and the burial service was conducted by the neighboring minister. He left a young widow about twenty-three years of age, named Cecilia, called Siselye, and a daughter Mary, two years of age, and Margaret, an infant.

Pooley asserted that a few days after the funeral he courted the widow, and was encouraged, but afterward she accepted the attentions of William Ferrar, a neighbor, and brother of the Deputy Governor of the Virginia Company in London. The affair caused a great deal of gossip, and Governor Wyatt referred Pooley's complaint of breach of promise to the London Company. In the Company's *Transactions* is the following minute, under date of April 21st, 1624: "Papers were read, whereof one containing certain examinations touching a difference between Mr. Pooley and Mrs. Jordan, referred unto the Company here for answer, and the Court requested to confer with some civilians, and advise what answer was fit to be returned in such a case." A few months later the Governor of Virginia

2

issued the following order against flirting:
"Whereas, to the great contempt of the
majesty of God and ill example to others,
certain women within this colony have, of
late, contrary to the laws ecclesiastical of
the realm of England, contracted themselves to two several men at one time,
whereby much trouble doth grow between
parties, and the Governor and Council of
State much disquieted. To prevent the
like offense to others hereafter, it is by the
Governor and Council ordered in Court that
every minister give notice in his church, to
his parishioners, that what man or woman
soever shall use any words or speech tending to the contract of marriage, though
not right and legal, yet so may entangle
and breed struggle in their consciences,
shall for the third offense undergo either
corporal punishment, or other punishment

by fine or otherwise, according to the guilt
of the persons so offending."

Poor Pooley at last found a woman to
love and be his wife, but in 1629 he and
his family were massacred by the Indians.

### MR. FENTON.

At Elizabeth City, on the 5th of September, 1624, a Rev. Mr. Fenton was buried,
who had recently arrived.

### HENRY JACOB.

Henry Jacob, the eminent scholar and
writer, and founder of the first Independent
Church in London, was induced to come to
Virginia, about 1624, and soon died. It is
supposed that he may have gone to the
Puritan plantations of Warasquoyak,
established by Edward Bennett and other
London merchants, and perhaps succeeded
William Bennett.

---

# CHAPTER III.

## CLERGY FROM A.D. 1630 TO A.D. 1660.

### WILLIAM COTTON.

William Cotton is the second minister residing on the eastern shore of Chesapeake
Bay, and may have been the immediate
successor of Robert Bolton, whom we have
noticed. It was a law of the colony "that
whosoever should disparage a minister without sufficient proof to justify his reports,
whereby the minds of his parishioners
might be alienated from him, and his ministry prove the less effectual, should ask the
minister forgiveness, publicly, in the congregation."

Henry Charlton, who, at the age of nineteen, came in 1623 to Virginia, and was a
servant of a planter in Accomac, Captain
John Wilcocks, one day in 1633 called the
Rev. Mr. Cotton "a black-coated rascal,"
and it was ordered by the County Court,
"that Mr. Henry Charlton make a pair of
stocks, and sit in them several Sabbath

days, during divine service, and then ask
Mr. Cotton's forgiveness for using offensive
and slanderous words concerning him."

Stephen Charlton, who left, on certain
conditions, property to the Episcopal Church
in Northampton, or lower Accomac, was
probably the son of this offender.

### MR. FALKNER.

Mr. Falkner, in the proceedings of the
Assembly of 1643, is mentioned as the
rector of the large parish of the Isle of
Wight county, but we find no further record
of his life.

It was not until after the year 1630 that
the colonists of Virginia began to increase
in wealth and population. In May, 1630,
the population of the Colony was reputed
to be twenty-five hundred. But in five
years it had doubled. In 1636 twenty-six
ships arrived, bringing sixteen hundred

and six immigrants. After this period there was some improvement in architecture.

The Virginia planters, in a document written in 1623, state ' that the houses were most built for use and not for ornament." The laboring men's houses in England, to which class they say " We chiefly profess ourselves to be, are in no wise generally, for goodness, to be compared unto them."

To stimulate improvements, in 1638 the authorities at Jamestown offered land for a house and garden to any who would build a dwelling.

In 1640 twelve houses were built, one of brick, owned by Secretary Kemp, and considered the "fairest in the Colony," and at the same time the first brick church in Virginia, twenty-eight by fifty-six feet in size, was commenced at Jamestown. Many years afterwards, A. D. 1676, it was destroyed by fire, and another church, the ruins of which are still seen, was erected.

A levy of tobacco, at the same period, was ordered, to repair Point Comfort and build a State-house at Jamestown, and Menefie, sometimes spelled Menify, a prominent merchant, was sent to England to dispose of the tobacco and procure workmen.

### ANTHONY PANTON.

Anthony Panton was the most prominent of the Virginia clergy, from the beginning of the reign of Charles the First until the death of Charles the Second.

At the solicitation of George Menify, a prominent man in Virginia affairs, and others, Panton, in 1633, came to America.

Menify had arrived in July, 1623, in the ship "Samuel," and became, in a few years, a prosperous merchant of James City corporation, and agent for London merchants. He lived on a plantation called Littleton, between Jamestown and Warwick river, and his surroundings were more refined than the other colonists. He was the first person who raised peach trees in the valley of James river, and gave great attention to horticulture. His garden of two acres was full of primroses, sage, marjoram and rose-

mary, and also contained apple, cherry, pear and peach trees. Panton's field of labor was in the new plantation of York, and the parish of Chiskiak, created 1639-40 by the legislature.

In 1629 a law relative to the observance of the Sabbath was reënacted in these words : 'That there be an especiall care taken by all commanders and others that the people doe repaire to their churches on the Saboth day, and to see that the penalty of one pound of tobacco for every time of absence, and fifty pound of tobacco for every month's absence, sett down in the act of the Generall Assembly, 1623, be levyed, and the delinquents to pay the same, as also to see that the Saboth day be not ordinarily profaned by working in any imployments, or by journeying from place to place."

About the time of Panton's arrival, in view of the scarcity of ministers, the legislature enacted : " In such places where the extent of the care of any mynister is so large that he cannot be present himself on the Saboth dayes and other holy dayes. It is thought fitt, That they appoynt and allow mayntenance for deacons, where any having taken orders can be found, for the readinge common prayer in their absence."

The Virginians had been indignant at the intrusion of Governor Calvert upon one of their plantations in Chesapeake bay, which had sent a representative to the legislature at Jamestown, and when one of their citizens, of the isle of Kent, had been killed in a collision with Marylanders, they became indignant at Governor Harvey's sympathy with those whom they considered intruders, and on the 27th of April, 1635, a meeting of influential persons was held at the York plantations, to adopt measures of redress for the many grievances they had suffered from their Governor. The next day a meeting of the Council was held at Jamestown, and after excited discussion, Governor Harvey was arrested for treason, and sent over to England. The following December, at a meeting of the king's Privy Council, it was charged that one Rabnet, of

Maryland, had said that it was lawful and meritorious to kill a heretic king, which was offered to be proved by one Mr. Williams, a minister, but Governor Harvey refused his testimony, because he married two persons without a license.

Another charge was that he had silenced a minister by the name of White.

To this Governor Harvey answered that White, in two years' time, had never shown any orders.

Archbishop Laud, who was present at the examination, sustained Harvey, by saying, "that no man may be admitted to serve as a Minister in any of the King's ships, until he has shown his orders to the Bishop of the Diocese."

Harvey was upheld by the King, and reappeared in Jamestown in 1637, with increased authority, and the increased dislike of the Virginians. The Secretary of the Colony and warm sympathizer with the Governor was Richard Kemp.

Acting both as accuser and judge, in 1638, Kemp charged Anthony Panton, Rector of York and Chiskiack, with calling him "a jackanapes ; that the King was misinformed, and that he was unfit for the place of Secretary, that he was poor and proud, with hair-lock tied up with a ribbon as old as Paul's," and also that he had preached against his pride; upon these charges, Harvey banished the minister for "mutinous, rebellious and riotous actions."

Panton complained to the King's Privy Council. Harvey was soon removed from office and his successor, Governor Wyatt, was ordered to inquire into the Panton difficulty.

Before he could enter upon the examination, Kemp, without permission, sailed for England, and Thomas Stegg, of Westover, an influential merchant, who was once Speaker of the Assembly, was fined 50 pounds sterling and to be imprisoned during the Governor's pleasure, for aiding and assisting him to go out of the country, and furnishing him with money, because it endangered the colonial records, some of which he had carried away, and because he exhibited

contempt toward the Governor in refusing to answer Panton's counsel. In April, 1641, the Privy Council having heard both Kemp and Panton, the sentence against the minister was removed. On the 30th of October, Anthony Panton, calling himself "Clerk and Minister of God's Word in Virginia, and Agent of the Church and Clergy there," presented a petition to the House of Lords, in which he complained of the conduct of Governor Harvey, Secretary Richard Kemp and others, at whose hands the colonists had suffered many arbitrary and illegal proceedings, in speedy trial, extortionate and most cruel oppressions which have extended to unjust whippings, cutting of ears, fines, confinement of honest men's goods, peculation, and the supporting of Popery. He also stated that Kemp had secretly fled from Virginia, carrying away the charter and divers records, and with his associates had, by misrepresentations to his Majesty relative to Governor Francis Wyatt, who had only served under his last commission eighteen months, obtained a new government and a new charter.

After the reading of these complaints, it was ordered by the House of Lords that the new Governor, Sir W. Berkeley, Kt., Richard Kemp and Christopher Wormsley be stayed their voyage, and forthwith answer to the charges of the petitioner. Berkeley's commission as Governor had been signed in August, but owing to this and other delays he did not, before February, 1642, enter upon his duties in Virginia.

JAMES, KNOWLES, AND TOMPSON, PURITANS.

While Laud in England was having the "Book of Sports" read in the churches, and the youth, on Sunday afternoons, were encouraged to engage in games and dances, and the Court on Sunday evenings were at balls, plays, and masquerades, the Virginia Legislature, in March, 1643, enacted: "For the better observation of the Saboth, no person or persons shall take a voyage upon the same, except it be to Church, or for other cause of extreme necessities, upon the penaltie of the forfeiture, for such offence, of twenty pounds."

It had already, in 1629, been ordered "that the Saboth day he not ordinarily profaned by workeing in any imployments."

The assembly of 1643 provided for the spiritual independence of the parishes outside of James City, by a law, which gave to the vestry of a parish and the county commissioners the right to elect and make choice of their ministers, which ministers should not be suspended by the Governor, except by complaint made by the vestry, and that final removal from the parish pulpit was to be left to the Legislature.

In the summer of 1641 the minister of the large parish of Upper Norfolk, afterward Nansemond county, signified his intention to leave. In May, 1642, a letter was written and signed by Richard Bennett, Daniel Gookin, John Hill, and others, "to the pastors and elders of Christ Church in New England," which was carried to Boston by Philip Bennett, one of the best men of Virginia, and contained a request for three pastors to occupy parishes which had been created by the legislature a few weeks before.

The act was in these words: "For the better enabling the inhabitants of this colony to the religious worship and service of Almighty God, which is often neglected and slackened by the inconvenient and remote vastness of parishes,

"*Resolved*, That the county of Upper Norfolk be divided into three distinct parishes, viz't.: one on the south side of Nansimum river, from the present glebe to head of said river, on the other side of the river the bounds to be limited from Cooling's Creek, including both sides of the creek, upward to the head of the western branch, and to be nominated the South Parish.

"It is also thought and confirmed that the east side of Nansimum river, from present glebe downward to the north of said river be a peculiar parish, to which the glebe and parsonage house that now is shall be appropriated and called East Parish. The third parish to begin on the west side of Nansimum river, to be limited from Cooling's creek, as aforesaid, and to extend downward to the mouth of the river, including all Chuckatuck on both sides, and the Ragged Islands, to be known by the West Parish."

The request was prayerfully considered by the churches and ministers of Boston and vicinity, and three good men offered themselves—John Knowles, pastor at Watertown, and a ripe scholar from Immanuel, Cambridge; William Tompson, minister at Braintree, who had graduated at Oxford in 1619; and Thomas James, for two years the minister at Charlestown, and then removed to New Haven.

Early in 1643 they arrived at Jamestown, bearing a letter of introduction from Governor Winthrop to Governor Berkeley. They were coldly received, and Thomas Harrison, as Chaplain, used his influence to have them silenced, and thus prevented from preaching in the churches; but Winthrop, in his journal, says, "Though the State did silence the ministers because they would not conform to the order of England, yet the people resorted to them in private houses, to hear them."

Knowles and James returned after a few months, but Tompson, of "tall and comely presence," remained longer." Mather, in a commemorative poem, alludes to his success in Virginia—

"A constellation of great converts there
　　Shone round him, and his heavenly glory
　　　　wear;
　　Gookin was one of them; by Tompson's
　　　　pains,
　　Christ and New England a dear Gookin
　　　　gains."

Daniel Gookin was the son of the Daniel Gookin, of County Cork, Ireland, who in 1621 commenced a plantation at Newport's News. The father and son were both natives of Kent County, England. In 1637

Daniel Gookin, Sr., obtained a grant of twenty-five hundred acres upon the branch of Nansemond river, and in 1642 he was president of the county court there, and one of those who invited the ministers from New England, and by Tompson's preaching his son Daniel, about twenty-five years old, became a member of the Church, and in 1644 went to Boston to reside. Here he became a man of influence, a friend of Eliot, the missionary and superintendent of Indian affairs. He died in March, 1687, aged seventy-five years, and his tombstone is still seen in the graveyard at Cambridge. Sewall, the Chief Justice of Massachusetts, visited him when dying ; in his diary he calls him " a right good man." His descendants were very numerous.

### THOMAS HARRISON, D.D.

Thomas Harrison first appears in Virginia as the chaplain of Governor Berkeley. He was a man of learning, eloquence and pathos, and upon his arrival a strict conformist to the Canons and liturgy of the Church of England.

On the 13th of April, 1644, there was a naval engagement between a ship whose captain adhered to the cause of Charles the First, and two ships whose officers were in sympathy with Parliament. The divisions and strifes caused by the civil war in England had been noticed by the Indians, and on the 18th, a black Good Friday in the Colonial calendar, the savages suddenly swarmed around the feeble settlements in the Valley of the James River, and as quickly disappeared, with their hands full of reeking scalps. Strong men fainted with horror, some mourned and refused to be comforted, for their children were not, and all felt it was a heavy judgment.

From this time Harrison was a changed man. His sermons became more solemn and spiritual. He expressed his regret that, while keeping a fair exterior to the ministers from New England, he had quietly used his influence to have them silenced.

The Act passed by the legislature soon after the massacre had his full sympathy, and indicates a reviving of religious life. It is as follows :—

"Be it enacted by the Governour, Counsell, and Burgesses of this present Grand Assembly, for God's glory, and the publick benefitt of the Collony, to the end that God might avert his heavie judgments that are now upon us. That the last Wednesday be sett apart for a day of ffast and humiliation, And that it be wholly dedicated to prayers and preaching. And because of the scarcity of pastors, many ministers having charge of two cures,

"Be it enacted, that such a minister shall officiate in one cure upon the last Wednesday of everie month ; and in his other upon the first Wednesday of the ensuing month. And in case of haveing three cures, that hee officiate in his third cure upon the second Wednesday of the ensuing month, which shall be their day of fast ; That the last act, made the 11 of January, 1641, concerning the ministers preaching in the forenoon and catechiseing in the afternoon of every Sunday, be revived and stand in force. And in case any minister do faile so to doe, That he forfeit 500 pounds of tobaccoe, to be disposed of by the vestrey for use of the parish."

The arbitrary and choleric Berkeley disliked Harrison's changed manner, and dismissed him, as too grave a Chaplain. He then crossed over to the parishes of Nansemond, whose ministers he had helped to drive away, and preached to the people.

In October, 1645, the House of Commons ordered that there should be liberty of conscience, in matters of God's worship, in all of the American plantations. The next year Captain Sayle, afterward Governor of Carolina, and the venerable Patrick Copland, in his youth the friend of Nicholas Ferrar, and a preacher before the London Company in 1622, of a sermon which was printed with the title "Virginia's God be Thanked," left Bermudas with a party of sympathizers, and sailed to Eleuthera, a small isle of the Bahamas group, to establish a colony, where each person was to be at perfect liberty to worship as he pleased, without molestation from the State. The ship in which they embarked, when near their destination, struck upon a reef, and they lost much of their supplies. As soon as possible Captain Sayle built a pinnace, and with eight men steered for Virginia, and arrived there in nine days, and received succor from the Nansemond nonconformists. Finding that Governor Berkeley was bitterly opposed to Puritanism, Sayle proposed to Harrison that his parishioners should cast in their lot with Copland and others at Eleuthera, but the proposition was not accepted.

Among the " Winthrop Papers " there is a letter of Harrison, written at Elizabeth River, on the 2d of November, 1646, and sent to Boston by Captain Edward Gibbons, " the younger brother of the house of an honorable extraction," in which he writes that if the proposition had "found us risen up in a posture of removal, there is weight and force enough [in yours] to have staked us down again."

After this the Nansemond Puritans, upon the express condition that there would be a public legal acknowledgment of toleration in religion, migrated to Maryland and settled on the shores of the Chesapeake, near Annapolis. Harrison, in the fall of 1648, visited Boston, married a cousin of Governor Winthrop, one Dorothy Symonds, and returned to England.

On October 11th, 1649, the Council of State wrote to Governor Berkeley that they were informed by petition of the congregation of Nansemond, that their minister, Mr. Harrison, an able man of unblamable conversation, had been banished the colony because he would not conform to the use of the Common Prayer book, and as he could not be ignorant that the use of it was prohibited by Parliament, he was directed to allow Mr. Harrison to return to the ministry.

Harrison did not return to America, but became Chief Chaplain of Henry Cromwell, Lord Lieutenant of Ireland, and in Christ Church Cathedral, Dublin, he preached a sermon on the death of Oliver Cromwell, from the text, Lamentations, chapter v, verse 16th, which was published with the following title:—

" *Threni Hibernici; or, Ireland sympathizing with England and Scotland in a sad lamentation for the loss of their Josiah. Represented in a sermon at Christ Church, in Dublin, before his Excellency the Lord Deputy, with divers of the nobility, gentry and commonality there assembled, to celebrate a funeral solemnity, upon the death of the Lord Protector, by Dr. Harrison, Chief Chaplain to his said Excellency.*"

## THOMAS HAMPTON.

Thomas Hampton seems to have been the successor of Harrison at Jamestown; and in " Hening's Statutes " he is mentioned as consenting, in February, 1645, to the formation of a new parish called Harrope, including the Williamsburgh region. At a later period Wallingford was also set off from the old parish. Upon an old tombstone at Williamsburgh Bishop Meade found this inscription:—"The Rev. Thomas Hampton, Rector of this parish, in 1647."

## ROBERT BRACEWELL.

Robert Bracewell was elected a burgess to the Assembly of 1653, but it was ordered "that Mr. Robert Bracewell, Clerk, be suspended, and is not in a capacity of serving as a Burgess since, since it was unpresidential, and may produce bad consequences."

The obstacles to his taking a seat in the legislature cannot be ascertained. John Hammond, for seventeen years a resident of Virginia, in 1652 represented the Isle of Wight County in the Assembly, was expelled from that body and the colony, for libel and other illegal practices, and then went to Maryland, and from thence to England, where he appeared as a partisan pamphleteer in defense of Lord Baltimore and his officers in Maryland.

In a publication called ' Leah and Rachel," which appeared in 1656, and is reprinted in the Force Historical Tracts, he writes: "But Virginia, savouring not handsomely in England, very few of good conversation would adventure thither, as thinking it a place where the fear of God was not; yet many came, such as wore black coats, and could babble in a pulpit, roar in a tavern, exact from the parishioners, and rather, by their dissoluteness, destroy than feed their flocks."

He continued: "The country was loth to be wholly without teachers, and therefore rather retain these than to be destitute; yet still endeavors for better in their places, which were obtained, and these wolves in sheep's clothing, by their Assemblies were questioned, silenced, and some forced to depart the country."

## ROGER GREEN.

In July, 1653, Roger Green, minister of Nansemond, is spoken of as contemplating a journey to North Carolina. Francis Yeardley this year was a representative of Lower Norfolk County in the Legislature, and Green probably accompanied his brother, Argall Yeardley, this year, in his explorations to the Roanoke region. The Yeardleys were sons of the former Governor, and, as the Nansemond people, were Puritan in their sympathies.

## PHILIP MALLORY.

As early as the year 1644 a Mr. Mallory was rector of Hampton. In Hening's Statutes is the following Act of 1656 :—" For the encouragement of the ministers in the country, and that they may be the better enabled to attend both public commands and their private cures, It is ordered, that from henceforth each minister, in his owne person, with six other servants of his family, shall be free from publique levies, Allwaies provided they be examined by Mr. Philip Mallory and Mr. John Green, and they do certify their abilities to the Governour and Councill, who are to proceed according to their judgement." The Assembly of March, 1660–61 enacted, " Whereas, Mr. Philip Mallory hath been eminently faithfull in the minis-

try, and very diligent in endeavouring the advancement of all those meanes that might conduce to the advancement of religion in this country, It is ordered, that he be desired to undertake the soliciting of our church affaires in England, and there be paid him a gratuity for the many pains he hath alreadie and hereafter is like to take about the countrey's business, the sum of eleven thousand pounds of tobacco." In 1664 he was still rector of Hampton parish.

## SAMUEL COLE.

About the year 1650, in the absence of any vestry, Samuel Cole, Bishop Meade says, was appointed minister in one of the new counties of the Potomac, by the County Court In 1657 Mr. Cole was minister to the two parishes in Middlesex County.

## FRANCIS DOUGHTY.

Francis Doughty is mentioned as having preached in Lower Accomac, now Northampton. He was the brother-in-law of Willliam Stone, of Hungar's parish, who became the first Protestant governor of Maryland, and introduced the Puritans of Virginia to the shores of the Chesapeake in 1648, on condition that there was a law passed securing liberty of conscience.

Francis Doughty first lived in New England, then went to Long Island, and while there used to preach to the English in Manhattan, now New York City. His wife was the widow of Rev. John Moore.

After Stone became governor, Doughty resided in Maryland, and on Sunday, October 12, 1659, visited the Dutch Commissioners from Manhattan, who were dining at Philip Calvert's house.

The only letter extant of John Washington is one dated September 30, 1659, in which he tells the Governor of Maryland that he cannot attend the October Court at St. Mary, " because then, God willing, I intend to get my young son baptized. All of ye company and gossips being already invited."

Perhaps Doughty crossed the Potomac to perform the baptismal act for one of the pioneers of Westmoreland, Virginia.

Doughty's daughter first married Adrian Vanderdonk, a graduate of Leyden, a lawyer at Manhattan. After his death she became a wife of Hugh O'Neal, a planter on the Patuxent River, Maryland.

The Rev. Mr. Doughty at one time preached in Setlingbourne Parish, about ten miles from the plantation of John Washington, and there is extant a complaint against him, presented to the Governor by John Catlett and Humphrey Boothe, for refusing to allow them "to communicate in the blessed ordinance of the Lord's Supper," in which the complainants state that Doughty is a "nonconformist," and that on a certain occasion "he denied the supremacy of the king, contrary to the canons of the Church of England." A century later one George Washington, a relative of one of Doughty's parishioners, also denied the supremacy of the king.

## CHAPTER IV.

CLERGY FROM A.D. 1660 TO A.D. 1688.

Virginia, from the death of Oliver Cromwell until the accession of William and Mary to the throne of England, was largely given up to ignorance and riotous living. Berkeley was again made Governor in A. D. 1660, and retained the position until A. D. 1677. He hated the restraints of religion, indulged in profanity, and was the companion of the pleasure-loving Charles the Second. Having ejected hundreds of clergymen of Puritan sympathies from the pulpits of England, there were many vacancies for strict conformists to the Prayer-book, and few desired to go to the forests of America. Governor Berkeley's dislike of nonconformist ministers was also so great that they could not live in Virginia without molestation.

To the question of the English Government, propounded in 1671, "what course is taken about the instructing the people within your Government in the Christian religion, and what provision is there made for the paying of your ministry?" Berkeley bluntly replied, "We have forty-eight parishes, and our ministers are well paid, and by my consent, would be better, if they would pray oftener and preach less. But, as of all other commodities, so, of this, *the worst are sent us,* and we had few that we would boast of, since the persecution of

Cromwell's tyranny drove divers worthy men hither. But I thank God there are no free schools, nor printing; and I hope we shall not have, these hundred years; for learning has brought disobedience, and heresy, and sects into the world, and printing has divulged them and libels against the Government."

With a Governor and clergymen that did not command the respect of good men, yet laying stress upon the efficacy of its ordinances of baptism and the Lord's Supper, it is not strange that religious people began to hold meetings in their own houses, and place a low estimate upon any kind of ritualism, and listen to the preachers of the Society of Friends.

In 1663, John Porter was expelled from the House of Burgesses, because, in the language of the Act, he had been "loving to the Friends."

#### GEORGE WILSON, FRIEND.

The itinerant ministry of the Society of Friends, visiting from plantation to plantation, neatly attired, temperate in the use of meat and drink, appealing only to the New Testament, could but make a favorable impression upon the fair-minded; while it stirred up formalists of the Colony,

3

to cause the passage of a law, ordering "that all Quakers, for assembling in unlawful assemblages and conventicles, shall be fined, and pay, each of them there taken, two hundred pounds of tobacco."

George Wilson, a minister of the Society of Friends from England, was imprisoned, and there is preserved a letter, dated, "From that dirty dungeon in James Town, the 17th of the Third Month, 1662," in which he writes, " If they who visit not such in prison as Christ speaks of, shall be punished with everlasting destruction, O! what will ye do? or what will become of you, who put us into such nasty, stinking prisons as this dirty dungeon, where we have not had the benefit to do what nature requireth, nor so much as air to blow in at the window, but close made up with brick and lime?"

R. G., PERHAPS, ROGER GREEN.

About the time that the Colonial authorities were holding Friends, in Jamestown prison, a small quarto was published in London, in 1662, under the signature of R. G., entitled " Virginia's Cure; or an Advisive Concerning Virginia, Discovering the True Ground of that Church's Unhappiness." The writer thereof states that he had been for ten years a resident of Virginia, and he was, perhaps, Roger Green, who in Henry's Statutes is mentioned, in 1653, as Minister in Nansemond. R. G., in 1661, had returned to England, and in his pamphlet, the importance of concentrating the population of Virginia in two, the establishment of Fellowship in Oxford and Cambridge, for the supply of an educated ministry, and the appointment of a Bishop for Virginia, are earnestly urged. His representations made an impression, and a patent for the creation of a Bishop was drawn, and the Rev. Alexander Murray was nominated for the office, but difficulties arose, and the scheme was abandoned.

Speaking of the members of the Virginia Assembly, R. G. writes, they were "usually such as went over servants thither, and though by time and industry they may have attained competent estates, yet, by reason of their poor and mean condition, were unskillful in judging of a good estate, either of Church or Commonwealth, or the means of procuring it."

The immodest and immoral poetess, Aphra Behn, who lived at this period, in one of her plays, alludes to the above state of things, by introducing two friends at Jamestown, who converse as follows:—

" Hazard. This unexpected happiness o'erjoys! who could have imagined to have found thee in Virginia!

" Friend. My uncle's dying here left me a considerable plantation, * * * * * but pr'ythee what drew thee to this part of the new world?

" Hazard. Why, faith, ill company, and the common vice of the town, gaming. * * * * * I had rather starve abroad, than live pitied and despised at home.

" Friend. Would he [the new Governor] were landed; we hear he is a noble gentleman.

" Hazard. He has all the qualities of a gentleman; besides, he is nobly born.

"Friend. This country wants nothing but to be peopled with a well-born race, to make it one of the best colonies in the world, * * * * * but we are ruled by a Council, some of which have been, perhaps, transported criminals, who having now acquired great estates, are now become your Honor, and R't. Worshipful, and possess all places."

MORGAN GODWYN OR GODWIN.

Morgan Godwyn came to Virginia after the publication, and perhaps was stirred to leave his warm nest in England by the reading, of R. G.'s pamphlet. He was an earnest young student, about twenty years of age, when the essay was published, and belonged to a family of theologians. His great-grandfather was the learned Thomas Godwyn, Bishop of Bath and Wells. His grandfather, Francis, was the Bishop of Hereford, and his father, Morgan, Archdeacon of Shropshire. He entered Oxford in 1661, and received, on March 16th, 1664–5, the degree of A. B., and soon after came to Virginia. His residence in the Colony was not pleasant. He was horrified at the state of morals, and the abject condition of the Africans and Indians, who were treated with less consideration than the dogs of a planter's kennel. Returning to England, after sojourning for some time in the West Indies, he engaged in the crusade against slaveholders, which a century later was taken up by Clarkson and Wilberforce. In 1680 he published a dissertation called "*The Negroes' and Indians' Advocate suing for their admission into the Church, or a Persuasive to the instructing and baptizing the Negroes and Indians in our Plantations; showing that as the compliance therewith can prejudice no man's just interest, so the willful and neglectful opposing of it is no less a manifest apostasy from the Christian Faith.*"

Five years later he preached a discourse in Westminster Abbey, exposing the inhumanity of slaveholding, from the text, Jeremiah ii, 34. "In thy skirts is found the blood of the souls of the poor innocents: I have not found it by secret search, but upon all these." It was printed under the title of "*Trade preferred before Religion, and Christ made to give place to Mammon, represented in a Sermon relating to Plantations.*"

Under his influence, it is supposed that the law was passed by the Virginia Assembly of 1667, declaring that the baptism of slaves did not make them freemen; in order that, in the language of the Act, "divers masters, freed from this doubt, may more carefully endeavor the propagation of Christianity by permitting children, though slaves, or those of greater growth, if capable, to be admitted to that sacrament."

His description of religion in Virginia is startling. He writes "The ministers are most miserably handled by the plebeian juntos, the Vestries, to whom the hiring (that is the usual word there) and admission of ministers is solely left. And there being no law obliging them to procure any more than a lay reader, to be obtained at a very moderate rate, they either resolve to have none at all, or to reduce them to their own terms." In another place he asserts: "Two-thirds of the preachers are made up of leaden lay-priests of the vestries' ordination, and are both the shame and grief of the rightly ordained clergy there."

## THOMAS TEACKLE.

Thomas Teackle was the son of a royalist, who was killed in the war between Charles and the Parliament. He came to Virginia in 1656, and settled at Cradock, in lower Accomac, now Northampton County. He married Margaret, daughter of Robert Nelson, a merchant of London, and remained in that county until the day of his death, January 26, 1695. His son John, born September 2, 1693, married, in 1710, a daughter of Arthur Upshur, a gentleman whose house was open for Friends' preachers. The descendants of this early Virginia clergyman are wide-spread. The writer values the acquaintance of one of them, a lady of quiet culture and retiring disposition, one of whose parents was a Teackle, of Virginia, the other a lineal descendant of a graduate of Trinity College, Cambridge, Old England, and an early President of Harvard University, at Cambridge, in New England.

## EDMUNDSON, THE FRIEND.

William Edmundson, once a soldier in Cromwell's army, came to the Chesapeake with George Fox, the great leader among the Society of Friends. While the latter visited New England, Edmundson traveled in North Carolina and Virginia. In 1672 he visited Governor Berkeley, and in his Journal writes:—

"As I returned, it was laid upon me to visit the Governor, Sir William Berkeley, and to speak with him about Friends' sufferings. I went about six miles out of my way to speak with him, accompanied by William Garrett, an honest, ancient Friend. I told the Governor I came from Ireland, where his brother was Lord Lieutenant, who was so kind to our Friends, and if he had any service to his brother, I would willingly do it; and as his brother was kind to our Friends in Ireland, I hoped he would be so to our Friends in Virginia. He was very peevish and brittle, and I could fasten nothing on him with all the soft arguments I could use."

### JOHN CLOUGH OR CLUFF.

John Cluff was one of the ministers denounced by young Nathaniel Bacon in the civil war of 1676, for upholding Governor Berkeley. In the year 1680 he was Rector of Southwark, in Surry County.

### JOHN PAGE.

John Page was another clergyman denounced in 1676 by Bacon. In 1680 he had charge of all the churches in Elizabeth County. In 1687 he was in New Kent County, and in 1719 he was still alive and in Elizabeth County.

### MR. WADING.

When Bacon led the insurgents to Gloucester County, a minister named Wading refused to acknowledge his authority, and encouraged others to follow his example. Bacon placed him under arrest, telling him that it was his place to preach in the Church and not in the camp. In the Church he could say what he pleased, but in the camp he was to say no more than what should please Bacon, unless he would fight to better purpose than he could preach. The second in command under Major Laurence Smith, during the Bacon insurrection, was a minister, who, says a chronicler of the day, "had laid down the miter, and taken up the helmet."

### DUELL PEAD.

On the 16th of April, 1663, in the Westminster Abbey font, then newly set up, Duell Pead, one of the King's scholars, about sixteen years of age, was publicly baptized. He entered, in 1664, Trinity College, Cambridge. Ordained by the Bishop of Lincoln, in 1671, he was chaplain of H. M. Ship Rupert. In 1683 he came to Virginia, with Major General Robert Smith, remained seven years as a minister in Middlesex County, and then went back to England, and became minister of St. James, Clerkenwell. He died on the 12th of January, 1726, and was buried in the parish churchyard. He had a son, Duell, a graduate of Sidney College, Cambridge, in 1712, who became a minister and came to America. By the will of the senior Pead, some horses and cows were left to his old parish in Virginia.

### JOHN CLAYTON.

Buck, Harrison, Hampton, and Godwin, have been noticed as ministers at Jamestown. By a law of the colony, the appointment of a rector for this place was made by the Governor. Godwin asserts that, with brief intervals, Jamestown for twenty years was without a rector.

About the time that Godwin was preparing his discourse in England, on "Trade before Religion," John Clayton was the parson at James City. The following letter was addressed by him to the Christian philosopher, Robert Boyle :—

"VIRGINIA, JAMES CITY, June 23d, 1684.

"HON. AND WORTHY SIR :—In England, having perused, among the rest of your valuable treatises, that ingenious discourse of the Noctiluca, wherein, as I remember, you gave an account of several nocturnal irradiations; having, therefore, met with the relation of a strange account in that nature, from very good hands, I presumed this might not prove unwelcome, for the fuller confirmation of which I have enclosed the very paper Col. Digges gave me thereof, under his own hand and name, to attest the truth, the same being likewise asserted to me by Madam Digges, his lady, sister to the said Susanna Sewell, daughter to the late Lord Baltimore, lately gone for England, who I suppose may give you fuller satisfaction of such particulars as you may be desirous to be informed of.

"I cannot but admire the strangeness of

such a complicated spirit of a volatile salt and exalted oil, as I deem it to be, from its crepitation and shining flame: how it shall transpire through the pores, and not be inflamed by the joint motion and heat of the body, and afterward so suddenly be actuated into sparks, by the slacking or bursting of her coat, raises my wonder.

"Another thing, I am confident your honor would be much pleased at the sight of a fly we have here, called the fire-fly, about the bigness of the cantharides; its body of a dark color, the tail of it a deep yellow by day, which by night shines brighter than the glow-worm, which bright shining ebbs and flows, as if the fly breathed with a bright and shining spirit. I pulled the tail of the fly into several pieces, and every parcel thereof would shine for several hours, and cast a light around it.

"Be pleased favorably to interpret this fond impertinency of a stranger. All your works have to the world evidenced your goodness, which has encouraged the presumption, which is that which bids me hope its pardon. If there be anything in this country I may please you in, be pleased to command; it will be my ambition to serve you, nor shall I scruple to ride two or three hundred miles to satisfy any query you shall propound.

"If you honor me with your commands, you may direct your letters to Mr. John Clayton, parson of James City, Virginia.

"Your humble servant, and, though unknown, your friend,

"JOHN CLAYTON."

The writer appears to have returned to England and become Rector of Crofton at Wakefield in Yorkshire. In May, 1688, he prepared for the Royal Society an account of his voyage to Virginia, and the things worthy of observation, which, in 1708, was published at London. Another John Clayton, an eminent botanist and physician, when about twenty years of age, came in 1706 to Virginia, and in 1773 died, aged eighty-seven years. There was also a

third John Clayton some years before the Declaration of Independence, who was Attorney-General of the colony.

### WILLIAM SELLICK.

William Sellick was in charge of St. Peter's Parish, New Kent, in 1680.

### ROBERT CARR.

Robert Carr appears to have been officiating in New Kent for six years from A. D., 1680.

### THOMAS VICARS.

Thomas Vicars came to Virginia about 1677, and was connected with the parishes of Gloucester county for twenty years.

### JUSTINIAN AYLMER.

Justinian Aylmer, Bishop Meade states, was at Elizabeth City from 1667 to 1690, a period of twenty-three years, yet his name does not appear in 1680 among the Rectors of Virginia.

### JOHN SHEPPARD.

John Sheppard appears in Middlesex county as early as 1668, and in 1680 was in charge of Christ's Church parish. Sir Henry Chichely was one of his parishioners.

### MINISTERS 1675 TO 1685.

In addition to those we have enumerated, the following ministers were in Virginia between A. D. 1675 and 1685.

Rowland Jones, James City county, A. D. 1674 to 1688.

Paul Williams, Surrey county, A. D. 1680.

Robert Park, Isle of Wight county, A. D. 1680.

William Housden, Isle of Wight county, A. D. 1680.

John Gregory, Nansemond county, A. D. 1680.

John Wood, Nansemond county, A. D. 1680.

John Laurence, Warwick county, A. D. 1680.

William Nern, Norfolk county, A. D. 1680.

James Porter, Norfolk county, A. D. 1680.

Edward Foliott, York county, A. D. 1680.

John Wright, York county, A. D. 1680.

Thomas Taylor, New Kent county, A. D. 1680.

William Williams, New Kent county, A. D. 1680.

Michael Zyperius, Gloucester county, A. D. 1680.

John Gwym, Gloucester county, A. D. 1680.

Charles Davies, Rappahannock county, A. D. 1680.

John Wough, Stafford county, A. D. 1680.

William Butler, Westmoreland county, A. D. 1680.

John Farnefold, Northumberland county, A. D. 1680.

Henry Parker, Accomac county, A. D. 1680.

Benjamin Doggett, Lancaster county, A. D. 1680.

Cope D'Oyley, Elizabeth county, A. D. 1677 to 1687.

---

# CHAPTER IV.

LIFE AND TIMES OF JAMES BLAIR, D.D., FOUNDER AND FIRST RECTOR OF WILLIAM AND MARY COLLEGE.

After the death of Sir William Berkeley, Lord Culpepper, and Lord Howard, of Effingham, in succession, acted as Governors of Virginia, and, though noblemen in name, proved themselves corrupt and avaricious in practice.

During their terms of office there was a large accession of Scotchmen to the population of Virginia. Immediately after the battle of Bothwell's Bridge a number of the hardy insurgents were transported to America, and about the same time another element not quite so desirable. Luttrell, connected with the Government offices of London, writes, in his diary, under date of November 19th, 1692:—"A ship lay in Leith, going for Virginia, on board which the magistrates had ordered fifty lewd women out of the House of Correction, and thirty others who walked the streets after ten at night." In addition to exiled soldiers and bawds, there came, as a foil, men fit to mold a State, men of angular manners, provincial accent, warm hearts, strong minds, and religious principles, whose descendants yet remain a power in the Commonwealth.

In the year 1673 James Blair graduated at the University of Edinburgh, and in time became a Presbyter of the Episcopal Church in Scotland, without Episcopal ordination. Burnet, once Archbishop of Glasgow, who lived in Scotland from A. D. 1643 to 1688, asserts: "No bishop in Scotland, during my stay in that kingdom, ever did so much as desire any of the Presbyters who went over from the Church of Scotland to be reordained." Blair, for several years was rector in the parish of Cranston, in Edinburgh county, but relinquished his office, and in 1684 received from the Bishop of Edinburgh, the following certificate:—

"To all concerned. These are to certify and declare that the bearer hereof, Mr. James Blair, presbyter, did officiate in the service of the Holy Ministry, as Rector in the parish of Cranston, in my diocese of Edinburgh for several years preceding the year 1682, with extreme diligence, care and gravity, and did in all the course of his ministry behave himself loyally, peaceably and canonically; and that this is the truth, I certify by these presents, and subscribed with my own hand, the 19th day of August, in the year 1684."

When Blair, in 1685, arrived at Jamestown, he found the social condition the widest contrast to his native land, where the poorest cottager owned a well-thumbed Bible; had reasons for the faith that was in him; and although not clothed "in purple and fine linen," felt that—

"The rank is but the guinea's stamp,
The man's the gowd for a' that."

With no schools in the colony, the planters had grown up in ignorance, and were the tools of a few rich land and slave owners, who, in conjunction with the Governors, enriched themselves by oppressive fees and unjust taxation.

The religion which Blair had learned taught him to think of the common people, and that his calling as a minister of the Gospel would be a failure if their elevation was not secured. His policy, and those of the oligarchy who came to Virginia to grow rich suddenly, did not harmonize, and great heat arose from the contrariety.

When he landed in Virginia he found Thomas Teackle, of lower Accomac, James Sclater, Duel Pead, Jonathan Saunders, Cope D'Oyley, Rowland Jones, and a few other clergymen in the Colony, but they did not possess the "perfervidam vim Scotorum" by which he was characterized.

In 1689 he was appointed the representative of the Bishop of London, with the title of Commissary, but with no power to confirm or ordain.

As a Scotchman, he could not rest until school-teachers were in the land, and he kept up an agitation for a college, both in private and public conferences, until he overcame the objection that education would take planters off from their mechanical employments, and make them grow too knowing to be obedient and submissive. Proceeding to England, on February 8th, 1692-93, the charter for William and Mary College was duly signed, and he and three other clergymen, John Farnefold, Stephen Fouace, who afterwards returned to England, and Stephen Gray, were mentioned therein as among the original trustees. In the preamble to the statutes of the College, published at a very early period, in Latin and English, the condition of Virginia at that time is thus stated:—

"Some few, and very few indeed, of the richer sort sent their children to England to be educated, and there, after many dangers from the seas, and enemies, and unusual distempers occasioned by the change of country and climate, they were often taken off by small-pox and other diseases. It was no wonder if this occasioned a great defect of understanding, and all sorts of literature, and that it was followed with a new generation of men, far short of their forefathers, which, if they had the good fortune, though at a very indifferent rate, to read and write, had no further commerce with the muses, or learned sciences, but spent their life ignobly with the hoe and spade, and other employments of an uncultivated and unpolished country."

Blair, upon his return, was appointed rector of the college, and turned his energies toward the erection of a building at the point afterward known as Williamsburgh. From this time the number of Scotch clergymen increased in the parishes. In 1696 there were ministers with these names: Francis Fordyce, John Alexander, Christopher Anderson, George Robinson, Andrew Monro, John Monro, Blair's brother-in-law, and Andrew Cant, who may have been the son of Andrew Cant, the Presbyterian zealot, who was Professor of Latin, and the parish minister of Aberdeen, handed down to posterity in the well-known lines—

"From Dickson, Henderson and Cant,
Apostles of the Covenant,
Almighty God deliver us."

Andrew, his son, entered the Scotch Episcopal Church, in time became the Bishop of Glasgow, and in 1728 died.

The downright earnestness and strong convictions of Blair roused opposition among the clergy and politicians. Sir Edmund Andros, who was made governor of Virginia, after leaving a memory by no means fragrant in New England, suspended him from the Council, because of his alleged restless "conduct," and the clergy in sympathy with the governor, opposed him because he did not carry on affairs in the high and dry way of the old English rectors.

Nicholas Moreau, a minister of French parentage, on the 12th of April, 1697, writes to the Bishop of Lichfield: "Your clergy in these parts are of very ill example; no discipline nor canons of the Church are observed. The clergy is composed for the most part of Scotchmen, people, indeed, so basely educated, or little acquainted with the executing of their charge and duty, that their lives and conversation are fitter to make heathen than Christians."

Not long before this letter was written, the wife of Commissary Blair was grossly insulted. Philip Ludwell, formerly secretary of the colony, had married the widow of Sir William Berkeley. By invitation Mrs. Blair was accustomed to sit in Lady Berkeley's pew in church. Colonel Daniel Parke, a gay, violent and dissipated man, had become much offended at a sermon which Eburne, the rector, had preached, upon the observance of the seventh commandment, as he had been faithless to his marriage vows. One day in ill humor, Parke went to church, and finding Mrs. Blair in the pew of Ludwell, who was his father-in-law, he rudely pulled her out.*

* Parke had been appointed by Andros Collector and Naval Officer for the Lower James River District. Leaving two daughters in Virginia, he was with the Duke of Marlborough in 1704, and was the Aid who brought to England the news of the victory at Blenheim.

Queen Anne made him Governor of the Leeward Islands; he was very unpopular, and on the 7th of December, 1710, was killed by a mob at Antegoa.

His daughter Lucy married Col. Wm. Byrd, and Fanny became the wife of John Custis, Collector of Customs in Accomac, a descendant of a Rotterdam inn-keeper.

The inscription on his tombstone indicates that he did not have much domestic felicity:

"Here, under this marble, lies the body of John Custis, Esq., of the city of Williamsburg, Parish of

A pasquinade printed in A. D. 1704, is very severe upon some of the clergy. Edward Portlock is lampooned as—

" The coxquean of the age :
A doughty clerk and reverend sage,
Who turns his pulpit to a stage,
And barters reformation :
    Rude to his wife, false to his friend,
A clown in conversation."

Jacob Ware, who, from 1690 to 1696 was minister of St. Peter's parish, New Kent, is portrayed as—

" Well warmed and fit for action ;
A mongrel parti-colored tool,
Equally mixed of knave and fool,
By nature prone to faction."

Ralph Bowker is stigmatized as—

    " A bawling pulpit Hector :
A sot, abandoned to his paunch :
Profane without temptation."

Soloman Whateley, another of the clergy, is—

    " A tool no person can describe :
Who sells his conscience for a bribe,
And slights his benefactors."

These lines were probably written by one of the friends of Governor Nicholson, who disliked Blair as much as his predecessor, Sir Edmund Andros. Nicholson was a Gascon in speech and manner. One night, while riding, he met the minister, Stephen Fouace, who came into the colony A. D. 1688, and ordered him not to visit a certain family. When remonstrance was made, the Governor said, excitedly, " When you came hither, you had more rags than bags!" The reply of the clergyman was: "It was no

Bruton ; formerly of Hungar Parish, on the Eastern Shore of Virginia, and County of Northampton, aged 71 years, and yet he lived but 7 years, which was the space of time he kept a bachelor's home, at Arlington, on the Eastern Shore of Virginia."

His son, John Parke Custis, married Martha Dandridge. When a widow, Martha Custis, she was married to the great George Washington.

harm to have been poor. The Governor then rode up and pulled his hat from his head, and asked how he had the impudence to ride in his presence with covered head.

The dispute between Governor Nicholson and Blair divided the colony into parties. Nicholson wrote to the Home Government concerning the Blair faction: "If they had the power of using the Scotch way of using the thummikins, or the French way of the rack, or the Barbary way of impaling or twisting a cord about peoples' heads, to make them confess, they would scarcely find any to swear up to what they would have them." In another letter he writes of Blair: "He might have had a sort of spiritual militia, but into whom, no doubt, he would have endeavored to have infused some worldly principles, as that they might have enjoyed a comfortable terrestrial subsistence before they had endeavored to have secured themselves a celestial habitation."

Blair, in 1705, was relieved of Nicholson's abuse, by his recall and the appointment of Edward Nott as deputy of Earl of Orkney, Governor.

By the year 1700 a number of French clergymen had been licensed by the Bishop of London to preach in Virginia, and we find the names of Moreau, Boisseau, Bartell and Lewis Latané, the ancestor of the esteemed Presbyter of the Reformed Episcopal Church who bears the same name.

The inhabitants divided into parties upon questions of public policy, leading to angry discussion and social alienation, many of the clergy preaching for the love of money, rather than constrained by the love of Christ, it is not surprising that plain people began to attach themselves to the Society of Friends, whose ministers accepted no compensation, and that not a few in high places were influenced by their earnest declarations concerning the love of Christ for sinners.

Before Blair left the University of Edinburgh, Richard Bennett, who had been Governor of Virginia, a man of wealth and influence, had sympathized with the

Friends in his neighborhood in Nansemond county, one of whom was John Copeland, whose ear had been cut off in Boston in 1658, as a disturber of the peace.

In A. D. 1698 there appeared another disciple of Fox in Virginia, named Thomas Story, a brother of the Dean of Lismore, of the Church of England and Ireland, fully the equal of Blair in culture, scholarship, and logical acumen. Toward the close of 1698, O.S., he held the first Friends' meeting at Yorktown. Two days later he was at the house of Thomas Cary, in Warwick, who, with his wife, had lately become Friends, and while visiting there, Miles Cary and his wife "were made partakers of the heavenly visitation."

Crossing the James river into Nansemond, he stopped at the house of the aged Copeland, whose single ear attested what he had lost and suffered for the faith, in Boston, forty years before. On the 10th of the Second month, 1699, he visited the Chickahominy village, of eleven wigwams, on Pamunkey neck, and then went one mile, to the house of a son of the distinguished William Clayborne, for many years secretary of the Colony. Two weeks later he preaches at the house of a Baptist minister in Yorktown, and from thence travels to Pocoson, where he found a large congregation, and was entertained by Thomas Nichols and wife, the latter, he says, in his journal, "though a mulatto by extraction, yet not too tawny for the divine light of the Lord Jesus Christ." At Kecoughtan, now Hampton, he tarried with George Walker, whose wife was the daughter of the once noted Quaker preacher, George Keith.

A second visitation was made by Story, in A.D. 1705. On the 26th of the Fourth month he was at Williamsburgh, conversing with Governor Nicholson upon the reasonableness of "all people that are of opinion that they ought to pay their preachers paying their own, and not exacting pay from others who do not employ nor hear them." Two days afterward he called at the house of Miles Cary, Secretary of Warwick

4

county. On the 5th of the Seventh month his traveling companion, Joseph Glaister, had a discussion with Andrew Monro, a Scotch clergyman, at the mansion of Colonel Bridges, at the south side of the James river. The weather being hot, Monro, who was an elderly man, became so faint and weary as scarcely to be heard; at length he called for a pipe of tobacco and a tankard of ale, and soon, on his part, the discussion "ended in drink and smoke."

Five days afterwards James Burtell, the French clergyman, came to the house of Thomas Jordan, a county judge, to hold a public discussion with Story, as to the baptism intended in the words of Jesus Christ: "Go ye, therefore, and teach all nations, baptizing them in the name of the Father, and of the Son, and of the Holy Ghost."

Burtell affirmed that water baptism only was commanded. Story argued that the baptism of the Holy Ghost was intended. "I grant," said the latter, "the apostles could not baptize with the Holy Ghost at their own pleasure, when and whom and where they would, in their own wills, as your ministers can and do administer what they call, and have taught you, Christ's baptism; but that the apostles could not instrumentally baptize with the Holy Ghost, I deny." * * * * At the same time he referred to the text, "Go ye into all the world and preach the Gospel to every creature. He that believeth and is baptized shall be saved; but he that believeth not shall be damned." And that this was not water baptism plainly appeareth, for Jesus said: "John truly baptizeth with water, but ye shall be baptized with the Holy Ghost not many days hence."

Story, also, declared that the baptism here spoken of was contra-distinguished from John's baptism, and could only be administered by the power of the Holy Ghost, co-working in them, with them, and by them.

These discussions caused the people to "search the Scriptures," and those clergy-men who did not lay stress upon the power of the Holy Spirit had but few hearers.

Blair, amid all of the distractions within his own branch of the Church, and the controversies caused by the presence of Friends' preachers, was studious and faithful in his sermons. At a Convention of the Episcopal clergy, in A.D. 1719, held at Williamsburgh, the question was considered, whether the Commissary had ever been Episcopally ordained? A majority voted that they had no evidence of the fact. The men who placed themselves on record upon this point, were Pownal, Seagood, Emanuel Jones, Lewis Latané, Bartholomew Yates, John Skaife, Hugh Jones, John Worden, John Bagge, James Falconer, Alexander Scott, and Ralph Bowker.

Yates was one of the most devoted clergymen in the Colony. Ordained at Fulham, by the Bishop of London, in A.D. 1710, he arrived in Virginia, and became the minister of Christ Church parish, in Middlesex county. He was chosen Professor of Divinity in William and Mary College, but still continued rector of his old parish, until July 26th, 1734, the day of his death. Not far from the Rappahannock river, in a deserted churchyard, is now seen the stone over his remains, erected by his parishioners, and the inscription thereon states that he was a tender husband, indulgent father, gentle master, and that "he explained his doctrine by his practice, and taught and led the way to heaven."

Lewis Latané, another respected minister, came to the Colony about the year 1700, and for twenty-three years preached in South Farnham parish, Essex county.

Emanuel Jones, of Petworth, Gloucester county, arrived the same time as Latané, and was a tutor of the college.

Skaife, who had been a curate in Cambridgeshire and Bedfordshire, came to Virginia, in 1708, and for many years had the charge of the parish of Stratton Major, in King and Queen county, and was one of the trustees of the college.

Bagge had been a curate in the diocese of Lismore, and in 1709 came to the Colony.

Hugh Jones arrived in Maryland 1698; about 1703 was elected Professor of Mathematics in William and Mary College. In 1724 there was published at London a duodecimo of one hundred and fifty pages, with the title, "The Present State of Virginia, and Short View of Maryland and North Carolina. By Rev. Hugh Jones, A.M., Chaplain to the Honorable Assembly, and late Minister at Jamestown, Virginia." The book contains the following description of the mode of worship during the term of Commissary Blair.

"In several respects the clergy are obliged to omit or alter parts of the Liturgy, and deviate from the strict discipline, to avoid giving offense, or else to prevent absurdities and inconsistencies. Thus surplices disused there for a long time in most churches, by bad examples, carelessness and indulgence, are now beginning to be brought into fashion, not without difficulty; and in some parishes where the people have been used to receive the communion in their seats, a custom introduced for opportunity for such as were inclined to presbytery to receive the sacrament sitting, it is not so easy a matter to bring them to the Lord's table, decently, on their knees."

At the time of this publication, the college at Williamsburgh is described as "without a chapel, without a scholarship, without a statute." On the 28th of June, 1732, the College chapel was opened by President Blair, preaching a sermon from Proverbs xxii, 6. "Train up a child in the way he should go, and when he is old he will not depart from it." A year later the foundation for the President's house was laid, the President and each of the faculty laying one of the first five bricks.

About the year 1700 the African population began to increase. Governor Nicholson writes in July of that year, that negroes were bringing "from twenty-eight to thirty guineas a head," and adds, "I believe two thousand would sell." In 1712

the Governor of Virginia announced that one-half of the population capable of bearing arms was composed of negroes and indentured servants.

In the Legislature of 1722-23 a law relative to suffrage was passed, which caused some discussion.

For almost a half century after the settlement at Jamestown universal suffrage prevailed, but in 1653 it was limited to "all housekeepers, freeholders, leaseholders or tenants," but two years after universal suffrage was restored, with the proviso that the votes were to be given by subscription instead of *viva voce*, and the Act was prefaced with a preamble stating that the Assembly conceived "it something hard and unagreeable to reason that any persons shall pay taxes and have no votes in election."

After the restoration of monarchy in England, and the return of Sir William Berkeley to the governorship, suffrage was again restricted to freeholders and householders. The preamble of the Act of 1670 is in these words:—

"Whereas the usual way of choosing burgesses by the votes of all persons, who, having served their time, are freemen ; who having little interest in this country, do oftener make tumults at the election, than by making choice of fit persons, and whereas the laws of England grant a voice in such elections only to such as by their estates, real or personal, have interest enough to tie them to the endeavor of the public good ;" then followed the restrictive clause, already alluded to.

In a few years the republican feeling was strengthened by Bacon and others, and in 1676 the restrictive clause was revoked, and universal suffrage again became the law of the land.

Eight years pass, and in 1684 it is again enacted that none but freeholders should exercise the right of suffrage. It was not until more than a hundred years after the meeting of the first legislative assembly that any effort was made to prevent the voting of Indians or free negroes. The Assembly of 1722-23, however, enacted that " no free negro, mulatto, or Indian whatsoever shall have any vote at the election of burgesses or any other election whatsoever." As required, the statutes passed by this Assembly were sent over to England for approval by the Commissioners of Trade and Plantations, and they were referred to their attorney, Richard West, afterward Lord Chancellor of Ireland, for examination. He reported adversely to the restrictive suffrage, using this language, " I cannot see why one free-man should be used worse than another, merely upon account of his complexion."

But, notwithstanding the opinion of the jurist, the Commissioners allowed the law to exist. When George Mason drew the first Declaration of Rights in America, which was adopted by the Virginia Convention in June, 1776, as part of their first Constitution, he reincorporated the idea set forth in the Suffrage Law of 1656, that it was "something hard and unagreeable to reason that any persons shall pay taxes and have no votes in election."

The sixth Article of the Declaration of Rights was in these words:—

"That elections of members to serve as representatives of the people in the Legislature ought to be free, and that all men having sufficient evidence of permanent, common interest with, and attachment to, the community, have the right of suffrage, and cannot be taxed or deprived of their property for public uses without their own consent, or that of their representative so elected, nor bound by any law to which they have not in like manner assented, for the common good."

Amid all the distractions of an active life, Commissary Blair found time to prepare one hundred and seventeen discourses on the sermon on the Mount, which were first published in London, in five octavo volumes. Dr. Doddridge, the Scripture expositor, pronounced it the best commentary on the fifth, sixth and seventh chapters of Matthew extant, and adds:—

"He appears to have been a person of the utmost candor, and has solicitously avoided all unkind and contemptuous reflections on his brethren. He has an excellent way of bringing down criticism to common capacities, and has discovered a vast knowledge of Scripture, in the application of them." A second edition of the work appeared in 1740, in four volumes, with a preface by Bishop Waterland.

George Whitfield, in his Diary, under date of 15th of December, 1740, writes:

"Paid my respects to Mr. Blair, Commissary of Virginia. His discourse was savory, such as tended to the use of edifying. He received me with joy, asked me to preach, and wished my stay were longer."

In 1743, after a ministry in Virginia of more than fifty years, he died, having proved himself an "emeritus miles," by "enduring hardness as a good soldier of Christ."

His son John, lived to see the independence of the United States of America, and to be one of the first judges of the Supreme Court, appointed by President Washington.

# CHAPTER VI.

LIFE AND TIMES OF JONATHAN BOUCHER, THE TORY CLERGYMAN, A.D. 1759–1775.

Jonathan Boucher was one of the best representative of the colonial clergy, from the period of ... the defeat of Braddock until the colonies declar'd themselves free and independent States.

He was born on the 12th of March, 1738 at Blencogo, in Cumberland county, England. While completing his education in mathematics, under the direction of a Rev. Mr. Ritson, who lived at Workington, near the mouth of the Derwent, he received an appointment as private tutor in the family of Captain Dixon, who lived on the Rappahannock river.

In July, 1759, he reached his destination at Port Royal. In his autobiography he writes: "Being hospitable, as well as wealthy, Captain Dixon's house was much resorted to, but chiefly by toddy-drinking company. Port Royal was chiefly inhabited by factors from Scotland, and their dependents, and the circumjacent country by planters in general, in middling circumstances. There was not a literary man, for aught I could find, nearer than in the country I had just left, nor were literary attainments, beyond merely reading or writing, at all in vogue."

In A.D. 1761, he was unexpectedly asked to enter the ministry. A Rev. Mr. Giberne, who lived on the north side of the Rappahannock, opposite Port Royal, about to marry a rich widow in Richmond county, resigned his parish, and the vestry asked him to fill the vacancy. He went to London, was ordained by Bishop Osbaldiston, and in July, 1762, became the rector of the parish in King George county, and preached at Leeds. In less than six months he was called to a parish near Port Royal, in Caroline county, made vacant by the death of the Rev. Thomas Dawson, Commissary of Virginia, which he accepted.

In the spring of 1763 he moved to this new field of labor, and remained seven years. Here he established a boarding school in his own house, and at one time had thirty pupils. Among his pupils was John Parke Custis, the step-son of General Washington. "This," says he, "laid the foundation of not a very particular intimacy and friendship, which lasted till we finally separated, never to unite again, on our taking opposite sides in the late troubles.

"Mr. Washington was one of those sons, of parents distinguished either for their rank, nor fortune. Lawrence, his eldest son, became a soldier, and went on the expedition to Carthagena, where, getting into some scrape with a brother officer, it was said he did not acquit himself quite so well as he ought, and so sold out.

"George, who, like most people thereabouts at that time, had no other education than reading, writing and accounts, which he was taught by a convict servant, whom his father bought for a schoolmaster, first set out in the world as Surveyor of Orange County, an appointment of about half the value of a Virginia Rectory, perhaps £100 a year.

"When the French made encroachments on the Western Frontier, in 1754, this Washington was sent out to examine, on the spot, how far what was alleged was true, and to remonstrate on the occasion. He published his journal, which in Virginia, at least, drew on him some ridicule. * * * * * At Braddock's defeat, and every subsequent occasion throughout the war, he acquitted himself much in the same manner as, in my judgment, he has since done, decently, but never greatly. I did know Mr. Washington well. * * * * * * * He is shy, silent, stern, slow and cautious. * * In his moral character, he is regular, temperate, strictly just and honest, and, as I always thought, religious, having heretofore been pretty constant, and even exemplary in his attendance on public worship in the Church of England. But he seems to have nothing generous or affectionate in his nature. Just before the close of the last war he married the widow Custis, and thus came into the possession of her large jointure. He never had any children, and lived very much like a gentleman, at Mount Vernon, in Fairfax County, where the most distinguished part of his character was, that he was an admirable farmer."

This estimate of Washington, from a Tory, can now be perused with complacency, since the world has long ago declared—

"He was a man; take him for all in all,
I shall not look upon his like again."

The French charged that Washington, under excitement, fired upon Jumonville, the French commander, while he was bearing a flag of truce. De Villiers, in his report of Washington's surrender at Fort Necessity, wrote:—

"We made the English consent to sign that they had *assassinated my brother*." In the articles of agreement it is so written. In 1756, these facts were brought to light by William Livingston, of New Jersey, and no doubt caused some criticism and ridicule of Washington.

Boucher, in one of his sermons, gives a picture of the bald and desolate appearance of the parish churches at the period of the Revolution. He remarks: "Our churches in general are ordinary and mean buildings, composed of wood, without spires or towers, or steeples or bells, and placed, for the most part, like those of our remotest ancestors in Great Britain, in retired and solitary spots, and contiguous to springs or wells. Within them, there is rarely even an attempt to introduce any ornaments; it is almost as uncommon to find a church that has any communion plate, as it is in England to find one that has not; in both Virginia and Maryland,

there are not six organs; the Psalmody is everywhere ordinary and mean, and in not a few places there is none."

Unlike Blair, he had no sympathy with Whitfield and his followers. Davies, more than his equal in eloquence, scholarship and spirituality, afterward President of Princeton, he looked down upon as a common dissenter. He used every means to prevent the growth of nonconformity, and in one of his sermons regrets its increase, and stated that thirty years ago there was not a dissenting congregation in Virginia, while then there were eleven ministers, and each with from two to four congregations.

In his autobiography he remarks, "I attributed much of my success in this (keeping down nonconformists), to my avoiding all disputation with their ministers, whom I spoke of as beneath such condescension, on the score of their ignorance and their impudence. And when one of them publicly challenged me to a public debate, I declined it, but at the same time set up one Daniel Barksdale, a carpenter in my parish, who had a good front, and a voluble tongue, and whom, therefore, I easily qualified to defeat his opponent, as he effectually did. And I am still persuaded that this method, of treating the preachers with well-judged ridicule and contempt, and their followers with gentleness, persuasion, and attention, is a good one."

Upon the subject of African slavery, he held the views of Henry, Jefferson and Washington. Destitute of moral cowardice, in 1763 he preached a sermon, in which he remarked—

"Were an impartial and comprehensive observer of the state of society in these Middle Colonies asked whence it happened that Virginia and Maryland, which were the first planted, and are superior to many colonies, and inferior to none in point of every natural advantage, are still so exceedingly behind most of the other British American Provinces, in all those improvements which bring credit and consequence to a country? he would answer: They are so, because they are cultivated by slaves. I believe it is capable of demonstration, that except the money interest which every man has in the property of his slaves, it would be for every man's interest that there were no slaves, and for this plain reason, because the free labor of a free man, who is regularly hired and paid for the work which he does, is in the end cheaper than the extorted eye-service of a slave. Some loss and inconvenience would no doubt arise from the general abolition of slavery in the Colonies, but were it done gradually, with judgment and good temper, I have never yet seen it satisfactorily proved that such injury would be either great or lasting."

During Boucher's residence in Caroline County, he manifested an interest for the slaves, and on the 31st of March, 1766, Easter Monday, baptized three hundred and thirteen negro adults, and preached to upwards of a thousand. He, moreover, employed two or three intelligent blacks to teach the children on Sunday afternoons. In time, twenty or thirty were able to use the Prayer-book at the Sunday services, and thirteen became communicants.

Calm and fearless in manner, logical and intellectual in his discourses, he succeeded in obtaining the entire respect of the planters among whom he resided. In one of his sermons he states that "he had lived among them more than seven years, as minister, in such harmony as to have had no disagreement with any man, even for a day." While in Virginia, he was intimate with the Rev. James Maury or Marye, a clergyman, of French parentage, born at sea, trained in England, educated in America, and settled in Albemarle county. At Maury's request, he wrote a poem, which was well received, on the dispute between the Clergy and the Assembly of Virginia, relative to the injustice of the act allowing two pence a pound to be paid instead of the 16,000 pounds of tobacco in kind, due as salary of a parish minister.

In 1770, he left Virginia, to become Rector of the church at Annapolis, the capital of Maryland, and took with him his pupil, John Parke Custis, the step-son of Washington.

The State House now used by the legislature of Maryland had not then been erected, and the church edifice was in a dilapidated condition, while the town boasted a handsome theater, in which Hallam and others played, built on land owned by the church. To stimulate his parishioners to the erection of a new church, he published, soon after he became the Rector of St. Anne's, in the Maryland *Gazette*, a poetical epistle, addressed:—

" *To the very worthy and respectable inhabitants of Annapolis, the humble petition of the old Church sheweth :—*"

A portion of this effusion is as follows :

" That late in Century the last,
By private bounty, here were placed
My sacred walls, and tho' in truth
Their stile and manner be uncouth,
Yet whilst no structure met mine eye
That even with myself could vie,
A goodly edifice, I seemed,
And pride of all St. Anne's was deemed.
How changed the times ! for now all round
Unnumbered stately piles abound,
All better built and looking down
On one quite antiquated grown :
Left unrepaired, to time a prey,
I feel my vitals fast decay ;
And often have I heard it said
That some good people are afraid
Lest I should tumble, on their head,
Of which, indeed, this seems a proof,
They seldom come beneath my roof.

\*　　\*　　\*　　\*　　\*

Here in Annapolis, alone,
God has the meanest house in town.
The premises considered, I,
With humble confidence, rely,
That, Phœnix like, I soon shall rise,
From my own ashes, to the skies ;
Your mite, at least, that you will pay,
And your petitioner shall pray."

While residing in Annapolis he determined to know something besides "Jesus Christ and Him crucified." He became much absorbed in the social, literary and political pursuits of the community. He wrote some verses on an actress, and a prologue for the theater, and was made first President of the Hominy Club, a society formed to promote innocent mirth. He was recognized as Governor Eden's right hand man and most intimate friend. He says: "I was, in fact, the most efficient person in the administration of Government. The management of the Assembly was left very much to me, and hardly a Bill was brought in which I did not either draw, or at least revise." The Governor's speeches, messages and other important papers were also from his pen. In the defense of what he supposed were the rights of the Maryland clergy, he had a sharp controversy with two lawyers, William Paca and Samuel Chase, both of whom, in 1776, were in the Continental Congress, and signers of the Declaration. Paca, smarting under some remark, was disposed to fight a duel with the rector of St. Anne's, but was quieted by the gentleman whom he consulted as his second.

Governor Eden, who valued his talents and friendship, in 1772 offered him the lower church of Queen Anne's Parish, Prince George county, Md., which he accepted. About this time he was married to a Miss Addison, a native of this county, niece of the Rev. Henry Addison, educated at Queen's College, Oxford, daughter of Thomas Addison, and grandchild of John Addison, Surveyor-General of the Province of Maryland.

His controversy with the lawyers, Paca and Chase, gave him a reputation among the Episcopal clergy of New York and New England, and King's College, now Columbia, in New York city, conferred upon him the degree of Master of Arts. The Rev. Dr. Cooper, President of King's College, visited him, and in company they proceeded to the residence of Rev. Dr. Smith, Provost of the College of Philadel-

phia, to concert measures to support the Mother Country in the pending controversies. "It is too well known," he says, "how little the clergy of Philadelphia regarded this agreement."

The ancestral residence of his wife's family was at Oxon Hall, nearly opposite Alexandria. In his reminiscences he writes:

"I happened to be going across the Potomac with my wife and some other of our friends, exactly at the time that General Washington was crossing it on his way to the northward, whither he was going to take command of the Continental army. There had been a great meeting of people, and great doings in Alexandria on the occasion; and everybody seemed to be on fire, either with rum or patriotism, or both. Some patriots in our boat huzzaed, and gave three cheers to the General as he passed us, while Mr. Addison and myself contented ourselves with pulling off our hats. Then General (then only Colonel) Washington beckoned us to stop, as we did, just to shake us by the hand, he said.

"His behavior to me was now, as it had always been, polite and respectful, and I shall forever remember what passed in the few disturbed moments of conversation we then had. From his going on his present errand, I foresaw and apprised him of much that has since happened; in particular, that there would certainly then be a civil war, and that the Americans would soon declare for independency. With more earnestness than was usual with his great reserve, he scouted my apprehensions, adding, and I believe with perfect sincerity, that if ever I heard of his joining in such measures, I had his leave to set him down for everything wicked. * * * * This was the last time I ever saw this gentleman, who, contrary to all reasonable expectation, has since so distinguished himself, that he will probably be handed down to posterity as one of the first characters of the age."

From this period, party feeling deepened in Maryland, and Boucher thought it prudent to leave his residence in the lower parish of Prince George county, and he removed to the "Lodge," the home of Rev. Henry Addison, his wife's uncle, in the upper part of the county. During his absence, services were held by his curate, a Republican, a brother of Robert Hanson Harrison, one of Washington's aids. He became increasingly unpopular, and whenever he preached there was more or less disapprobation. "For more than six months" he writes, " I preached, when I did preach, with a pair of loaded pistols lying on the cushion, having given notice that if any man or body of men could possibly be so lost to all sense of decency and propriety as to drag me out of my own pulpit, I should think myself justified before God and man in repelling violence."

In 1775 the Republican authorities set apart Thursday, the 11th day of May, for prayer and fasting, and Mr. Boucher announced that he would preach in his own pulpit. The text he had chosen was from Nehemiah vi, 10, 11 : "Afterward I came unto the house of Shemaiah, the son of Delaiah, the son of Mehetabeel, who was shut up ; and he said, let us meet together in the house of God, within the temple, and let us shut the doors of the temple, for they will come to slay thee ; yea, in the night will they come to slay thee. And I said, should such a man as I flee ? and who is there that, being as I am, would go into the temple to save his life ? I will not go in."

Fifteen minutes before the time of service he arrived at the church, but found the Republican curate, Harrison, already in the desk, and a crowd of armed men around the church. A Mr. Osborne Sprigg, who was the leader, told him that they did not wish him to preach. He replied that they would have, then, to take away his life ; and with sermon in one hand, and a loaded pistol in the other, moved toward the pulpit, but was instantly surrounded by excited men. Seizing Sprigg by the collar of his coat, and with cocked pistol, he told him he would blow his brains out if any of the crowd should dare attack him. The crowd, while not injuring him, forced him out of the church, and escorted him to his residence, a fifer playing the tune of the "Rogue's March." Fearless and persevering, he appeared at the church next Sunday, and, amid much confusion, preached the sermon he had prepared for " Fast-day."

From this time his feelings were embittered against the Republicans, and on the 16th of August, 1775, he wrote, under excitement, a long letter to Washington, which he concludes in these words :—

"I have, at least, the merit of consistency ; and neither in any private or public conversation, in anything I have written, nor in anything that I have delivered from the pulpit, have I ever asserted any other opinions or doctrines than you have repeatedly heard me assert, both in my own house and yours. You cannot say that I deserved to be run down, villified, and injured in the manner which you know has fallen to my lot, merely because I cannot bring myself to think, on some political points, just as you and your party would have me think. And yet you have borne to look on, at least as an unconcerned spectator, if not an abetter, whilst, like the poor frogs in the fable, I have in a manner been pelted to death. I do not ask if such conduct in you was friendly ; was it either, just, manly, or generous? It was not ; no, it was acting with all the base malignity of a virulent Whig. As such, Sir, I resent it ; and oppressed and overborne as I may seem to be, by popular obloquy, I will not be so wanting in justice to myself as not to tell you, as I now do, with honest boldness, that I despise the man who, for any motives, could be induced to act so mean a part. You are no longer worthy of my friendship ; a man of honor can no longer, without dishonor, be connected with you. With your cause, I renounce you."

In this frame of mind, he became odious to the friends of Congress, and in a month was a refugee.

On the 10th of September, with his wife and her uncle, the Rev. Henry Addison,

5

and his son, he went on board a small
schooner, the *Nell Gwynn*, and, sailing
down the Potomac, entered the Chesapeake,
and was taken aboard a vessel, which, on
the 20th of October, reached Dover, in
England. For nineteen years he was
Vicar of Epsom, and devoted much time to
philological studies. He died, A.D. 1804,
at the age of sixty-six years. His engraved
portrait shows a firm, benevolent, round-
faced man, with expansive forehead.

In 1797 he published "A View of the
Causes and Consequences of the American
Revolution," which he gracefully dedicated
as a kind of peace offering to his old friend,
who had been the first president of the
United States of America. Washington, in
reply to the compliment, in a letter from
Mount Vernon, dated 15th of August, 1798,
wrote, "For the honor of its dedication and
for the friendly and favorable sentiments
therein expressed, I pray you to accept
my acknowledgment and thanks. Not
having read the book, it follows, of
course, that I can express no opinion with
respect to its political contents, but I can
venture to assert beforehand, and with confidence, that there is no man in either
country more zealously devoted to peace and
a good understanding between the nations
than I am: no one who is more disposed to
bury in oblivion all animosities which have
subsisted between them and the individuals
of each."

He was married three times. His first
wife, Miss Addison, noted for her beauty,
had no children, neither had the second.
By his third wife he had several children,
one of whom was the Rev. Barton Boucher,
of Wiltshire. It was not until 1871 his
last child, a daughter, died. One of his
grandsons, bearing his name, is a valued
contributor to the London *Notes and Que-
ries*, and to him we are indebted for extracts
from his grandfather's journals.

In concluding this article, a brief refer-
ence will not be out of place, to Rev. Walter
Dulaney Addison, who became Rector of the
parish from which his uncle had been
ejected a few months before the Declaration
of Independence. He was the son of Thomas
Addison, whose wife was Rebecca Dulaney,
of Annapolis; and also the nephew of the
wife of Jonathan Boucher. In 1788, while
on a visit to his uncle, by marriage, in England, Mr. Boucher requested him to make a
catalogue of his library. In doing this, he
fell from a ladder while examining some
books on a high shelf, and was much injured.
While confined to his room he became very
serious, and determined to enter the ministry.
Returning to this country he married a Miss
Hesselius, of Annapolis, and then went to
reside with his mother at Oxon Hall, on the
Potomac. For several years he occupied
the same pulpits which Jonathan Boucher
had preached from in Prince George county,
and formed a wide contrast to his relative in
his views of religion. With what was considered Puritanic strictness, he frowned upon
duelling, horse racing, card playing, and
theater-going. While attached to the liturgy
of his Church, he maintained friendly rela-
tions with those whom he recognized as ministers of other branches of the Church. For
many years he was deprived of sight. God
took him, in 1848, ripe in age, and fit for
heaven. His friends deposited his remains
in the burial place of his ancestors, at Oxon
Hall.

# A PLAINT

OF SAMUEL PURCHAS, RECTOR OF ST. MARTIN'S, LUDGATE, LONDON, A.D., 1625.

---

" My prayers shall be to the Almighty for Virginia's prosperity, whose dwarfish growth after so many years' convulsions by dissensions, Tantalean starvings amidst rich magazines and fertilities, subversion here and self eversion there (perverseness I mention not), rather than conversion of savages, after so many learned and holy men sent there; poverty, sickness, death in such a soil and healthful climate—what shall I say?

" I can deplore, I do not much admire, that we have had so much in Virginia, yet so little; the promises as probable as large, and yet the premises yielding, in the conclusion, this Virginian sterility and meagerness, rather than the multiplied issue and thrift of a worthy nation, and mother of a family answering to her great inheritance. But what do I in plaints, when some, perhaps, will complain of my complainings?"

www.ingramcontent.com/pod-product-compliance
Lightning Source LLC
Chambersburg PA
CBHW021456090426

42739CB00009B/1754